FRY THE MONKEYS
CREATE A SOLUTION

The manager's and facilitator's guide to accelerating change
using Solution Focus

ALAN KAY

Fry the Monkeys Create a Solution:
The manager's and facilitator's guide to accelerating change
using Solution Focus

Published by: The Glasgow Group
179 Douglas Avenue
Toronto, Ontario
M5M 1G7, Canada
http://glasgrp.com

ISBN: 1456501895
EAN-13: 978-1456501891

TABLE OF CONTENTS

I. ABOUT THIS BOOK

1. Who should read this book?

Yes, the title was designed to grab your attention! We'll talk later about why we need to 'Fry' the monkeys (figuratively, not literally), on Page 8. In the meantime...

If you lead or facilitate change and people-growth and you like to stimulate purposeful dialogue in organizations, this book is intended to give you an additional tool for your work.

The intent of the book is not to prove that Solution Focus is the best thing going, only that it's a powerful way to help people in organizations create change – the change they want to see happening.

I urge you to continue using your current skill set and use Solution Focus to make the tools you use even better. My bet is that you will find, over time, that it's the most useful tool for your clients.

The theme of the book is that organizations will benefit from moving to solutions thinking because problem-focused thinking is an increasingly inefficient way to run an organization.

I am very grateful to the many colleagues that donated Solution focus recipes for you to practice. Through understanding the Ingredients (section II) and practicing these recipes (Section III), I am sure you will enhance the good work you are already doing in or for organizations.

2. Introduction

As Fletcher Peacock says, "Water the flowers, not the weeds." (Fletcher Peacock, B.Sc., M.S.W.). This is essentially the philosophy behind being "solution-focused."

Being solution-focused, we tend our garden by paying attention primarily to the flowers. The weeds go away because we don't water them. We simply ignore them.

We build on what's already working, explore what it would be like if the problem went away, and take small steps toward the things we want to happen.

Solution Focus is a simple, but not simplistic approach to achieve clarity and awareness about what is possible and to help initiate decision-making and movement. This approach is referred to as the "Solution Focus." This term and its approach will be explained in this book to empower you with recipes for change.

The Solution Focus approach is built on a solid foundation of more than thirty years of research and practical application from the world of family therapy. It is now a well-established approach for organizational change in the corporate and public sectors.

Solution Focus works because the participant engaged in the approach is the resource for change. As a foundational approach, the person who desires change for themselves or their organization figures out where they want to go and how to get the process started with your help.

3. Why creating a culture of solutions is important...

What's the primary benefit of solution-focused change in organizations? **Speed**. Taking time to use Solution Focus to audit existing resources, painting a picture of future success, and deciding on what to do first, creates decisiveness and speeds up movement toward change. It's that simple.

Wait, there's another benefit! **Resilience**, an often hidden asset of the organization gets better as a result of Solution Focus. Those experiencing success find the change **sustainable**.

And there's more: Solution Focus can help improve **productivity** because people decide what to do and take action by circumventing the low-productivity approach called indecisiveness.

A Solution Focus approach is counterintuitive to most of our thinking about change. To help the reader overcome these counterintuitive barriers, we will argue against, in this book, the Problem Focus that many organizations use in an attempt to make change happen.

Solution Focus brings out the best in an organization...literally. It has a positive effect on workplace culture, as well as people, systems, and processes. Solution Focus builds on the change and growth processes already used and complements existing capabilities. And it doesn't require a top-down effort to drive change.

What this book can do for you (and how you can use it)...

Applying Solution Focus in an organization is a bit like the way a chef might operate: use what's already in the kitchen and make something good happen by noticing and discovering the good ingredients you already have in front of you.

If you already have some familiarity with the Solution Focus approach, you may want to skip through the first section of this book. If you are skeptical about the claims herein, you may want to read about the understanding and theory behind Solution Focus in greater detail – you can find this information on the "resources" page 75.

Most of this book describes the ingredients and the recipes you'll need for cooking up Solution Focus. Finally, you can delve into a selection of kitchen-tested Solution Focus recipes that you can practice and adapt to your own way of working.

There are many approaches and tools available to grow and change an organization. They all have a useful effect in some way, but are they as easy to implement and sustain, especially when change is required across the organization? Are they flexible enough to help make change happen the way an organization wants?

This book urges you to build on the change skills you already possess. After reading, you'll find that you can modify your skills to integrate Solution Focus tools that make your work even more powerful.

4. Have you noticed the downside of Problem Focus?

You may find that an organization—even at an individual level—seems stuck in an endless loop of difficulty when trying to make changes. Anxiety, finger-pointing, and lack of willingness to take responsibility for change is often prominent.

Problem Focus is perfectly normal. People tend to talk a lot about the problem and a lot less about solutions. It is part of the human condition. We try to solve the vast number of problems we face by discussing them as though we have to understand them, in all of their complexity, in order to fix them. Engineers can. We people managers can't.

It is true that scientists and engineers make our lives safer by understanding physical and structural problems in the systems they create. This is done for our safety, to prevent the buildings or IT systems from collapsing. But in human systems, the workplace, examining the problem endlessly only serves to slow down change.

Talking endlessly about the problem is a bit like the chef discussing the problems in milk production, distribution, and marketing. There are endless problems in the process of bringing milk to the chef's kitchen. But does talking about them make the chef's recipe any better? Will a detailed understanding of how government subsidies drive up the cost of milk make the guests enjoy the soufflé any better? No.

Yes, we do have to identify and clarify the problems in our organizations. And we do have to learn to identify solutions, make informed decisions, and take action. Without the endless discussions about problems, think how much more productive we could be!

The Solution Focus approach is not an exercise in positive thinking and hiding from problems. It is about purposeful thinking to better understand what we need to do to make changes, and then actually making it happen.

Now, does Solution Focus advocate that we **never** talk about the problem? No. That's a form of denial. We still need to clarify the difficult issues. But we need to ask better questions about the problems we have and what we intend to do about them. Better questions often reveal there is less to worry about than we originally thought; they help clarify what we want to fix, and help define what we want to improve.

Ultimately, better questions reveal that we can be hopeful, even optimistic, about making progress right away.

If you want to test this notion, just try asking: "What happens when the problem isn't present?" or: "What would happen if the problem didn't exist?" At first, you'll need to be persistent in sticking with the question, but give it a try. It will create an entirely different perspective on achieving change.

We humans are really good at Problem Focus...

The answer may be self-evident, but why get beyond a culture of Problem Focus? Humans distinguish ourselves from other creatures by being exceptionally good at solving problems. We have been able to resist extinction by developing our brains in ways that prevent disasters and, more often than not, capitalize on threat. Over thousands of years we have thrived, often in hostile environments—think of the societies living close to the Arctic Circle despite daily threat from extreme weather and so on. The likelihood is that they thrived over time because they didn't have a lot of time to deliberate on what to do every time a problem arose. They were required to make choices without a lot of analysis and were, in the urgency of the situation, forced to think about what had worked before and what to do this time. Focusing on the details and the cause of the problem would have added little to their decision-making process.

So people living in hostile environments were forced to be what we would today call "creative" or "innovative". They would likely call it being practical and purposeful. In less physically hostile, but still complex, environments, we humans have distinguished ourselves from our distant cousins, the apes, by constantly noticing problems and creating solutions to them. We overcome difficulties, learn new approaches, and in the larger scheme of things, make progress.

The joy of being a scientist, an engineer, an architect, a mechanic

Scientists, engineers, and architects have always been successful at looking at problems. In fact, it's their job to eliminate problems from their project so that it will stand the test of time. In the absence of this process, many of our buildings and bridges would be susceptible to collapse. If the auto mechanics can't thoroughly examine your car's mechanicals they can't replace certain parts of the transmission in order to get you on the road again.

So what is wrong with the rest of us humans following the problem-focused path of the engineer or mechanic? Two things: 1) in human systems, versus engineering systems, rigorous analysis of the problem slows us down and prevents us from making decisions to move forward; 2) while the engineer has clear goals (this is the river and this is the bridge we will build to get across it), most people when focusing will unconsciously avoid thinking about goals and solutions. As a result, we greatly reduce the decision-making that is required to make progress.

Yes, I hear you saying, but if we don't explore the problem in the human system how will we know we have made the right decision? Well, how do you define the right decision? The engineer can identify the right decision because the system they are designing usually has a structure of some kind. Human systems, however, rely on a vast number of variables in behavior and attitude. Waiting for the "right" answer prevents us from seeing the obvious.

Now think of an organization; imagine the vast number of problems—simple and complex, strategic and tactical—that it faces every day. Because the organization has no way to control the outside world, external change creates ongoing internal complexity. Infinitely variable human behaviors and attitudes create internal and external friction. It is easy to see why people obsess about the problems around them. However, many of the problems are constructs created in the moment to express the difficulty in moving forward and making decisions. It seems easier to explore the "why" than how to assess the issues, explore change resources and opportunities, make decisions, and move forward.

Should we simply ignore the Problem Focus?

This is not to say that organizations do not need evidence to support decisions. They do, especially in an increasingly complex world. But in human behavior, causality-finding increases the likelihood of indecisiveness because there are too many variables to consider. Back to our chef: if the chef knows certain facts about milk (boiling point, fat content, and so on), but not the problems involved with getting the milk to the kitchen, she or he can still decide which way to use the ingredient.

A hidden issue in many organizations is the amount of time wasted discussing problems, finger-pointing, and attributing blame. It prevents decisiveness. Analyzing what has gone wrong inhibits people from asking what we actually want to do. And, when they do get to discuss what's required, the conversation is often quite thin.

Instead of capitalizing on opportunities, the conversation is weighted down by past process — processes that may not work when the future inevitably calls for change.

Experts are sometimes hired to help solve organizational problems and may inadvertently sustain the pain. How? Believing they are the equivalent of trauma counselors, they begin by examining the problem in detail. Having defined the problem, the experts then create strategies to solve it. In the process, the staff involved tries to make progress on the problem, but not necessarily the goals of the organization. Progress is undoubtedly made, but nowhere near the degree possible were the consultants to let go of being the experts in solving the problem.

Frying problem monkeys

'Fry' the monkeys? Let's remind ourselves of the story about the manager who is visited by three unhappy-looking staff members. The team is unhappy as they walk in to the manager's office because they have problems called monkeys chattering on their shoulders. Sometime later we see the staff leaving the manager's office looking relieved. Where are the monkeys? They are on the shoulders of the manager who has consciously, or not, decided to take on the monkeys. The manager has been somewhat derelict in his or her duties in two ways: one, it's highly inefficient for the manager to take on the monkeys presented by the staff; two, the manager failed to persuade the staff that their job is to bring solutions instead of monkeys.

Organizations take on an inordinate amount of problem monkeys. After all, many problems are a construct. It is assumed that once a problem has been identified and discussed, it is the truth. If a building is on fire, the problem is real, immediate, and it will do harm. If the organization has run out of cash, customers have stopped buying, or staff are leaving in droves, the problem is clear. Interestingly, denial often persists in this area, despite the clarity of the problem.

That said, the vast majority of problems are not nearly as concrete as people claim. The complexity of organizations tends to create angst — mountains of angst — which drives more anxiety. People assume that the problem can only be fixed by talking more about it, thereby making it concrete, but only in their minds. Very soon, as the perceived problems - the monkeys - pile one on top of the other, it is assumed that huge changes need to be made. Suddenly, the underlying assumption is that only systemic change will sort out the mess in which the organization finds itself.

So, how do we send the problem monkeys away?

It's about their unconscious resilience

We often fail to notice that we actually have the resilience to not only survive the problem, but also to achieve something purposeful. After all, we survived the problems that looked catastrophic at one point in the past.

Bypassing the reality that things are not nearly as bad as claimed is, in fact, one of the great strengths of human beings and their organizations —the ability to overcome adversity and make progress.

It does, however, sometimes encourage the notion that only heroic leadership can make things happen.

Creating an environment where solutions thinking abound does not assume that the problems will simply go away. It's about people learning to move on quickly and people becoming more decisive—the decision to do something is far better than no decision. It's about people working on their situational analysis using the facts they have, looking for insight beyond the information, and trusting themselves.

Does this also suggest there's something wrong with the formal approaches or systems organizations currently use to make change? No. They work well. But they are often system solutions, not people solutions. They don't build on people's resilience to deal with change.

So much for Problem Focus! What's the solution?

So, you're intrigued enough to want to know more. What do you do to encourage people to make the most of what's possible? There are many excellent books on how a Solution Focus approach works. This recipe book will show you how to apply a Solution Focus approach in organizations and maybe even your life.

Any group of people engaged in collectively making things happen can benefit from Solution Focus. It might be:

- a government department.

- a large, medium-sized or small shareholder-driven business.

- a public service institution, such as a hospital.

- a volunteer board of a not for profit charity or an association.

- a team.

- an individual.

These Solution Focus recipes work virtually anywhere. That might include the organization you spend your weekends with—your family and friends.

Situations where you might apply the Solution Focus recipes are to be found in section #37 on page 32.

The simple approach to Solution Focus

Solution Focus is counterintuitive. To reveal solutions—the ones staring us in the face—all we need to do is change the questions we ask. Let's repeat that:

> **All we need to do is change the questions we ask**
> **because ...**
> **in Solution Focus we simply ask better questions.**

- "A powerful question alters all thinking and behaving that occurs afterwards"—*Marilee Goldberg*

Solution Focus often asks counterintuitive questions. They sometimes sound unusual to the listener. They can be both difficult to ask and to answer. But, if you are prepared to be patient and fearless about trying this approach, you'll notice a difference right away.

- "The solution of the problem of life is seen in the vanishing of the problem"—*Ludwig Wittgenstein*

Solution Focus seeks to help people do something different about the problem so that it will go away.

How can you trust that Solution Focus will work for the team you are trying to assist? It is a deeply researched methodology. **Google the words:** solution focus, Insoo Kim Berg, Steve DeShazer, Ben Furman, Dr. Mark McKergow, Kirsten Dierholf, Peter Szabo and Coert Visser to get a better picture.

- "In the 1970's and the early 1980's, a startling discovery was made that almost every problem contains an element of solutions"—*Insoo Kim Berg*

Yes, I hear you saying, but we are more than a bit tired of quick-fix and fad change processes. Well, you'll just have to try this one.

- "The art of being wise is knowing what to overlook"—*William James*

And what if it doesn't work? Be brave. At the very least it won't do any harm.

- "Change is happening all the time ... our role is to identify useful change and amplify it"—*Gregory Bateson*

The rest of this book is about learning how to ask better questions. It's in the form of recipes. They include:

- The ingredients (or tools) required to make Solution Focus work for the team you are trying to help.

- Simple applications such as meeting tools. (The snacks)

- Applications for strategic planning and team coaching. (Full meals)

II. THE INGREDIENTS YOU'LL NEED

1. The ABCs of Solution Focus

Here's the DNA or the framework for the better questions asked in a Solution Focus approach:

A. What's working that we don't need to change?

B. Suppose we did more of that and the problem went away, what would be happening?

C. Suppose we got there; what would be the first small signs that we made progress?

Once you've mastered this approach you can simplify things to:

A. What's working?

B. What do we want?

C. What will we do first?

After you have memorized your ABCs, the next thing to remember is that you can use them in a sequence that works for the team:

B. What do we want?

A. What's working?

C. What will we do first?

A. What's working?

C. What will we do first?

B. What do we want?

The key to applying this approach is to remember that it's about the team's thinking, not yours. It's their skills, behaviors, and attitudes that they have to work with. Your skills, behaviors, and attitudes have to be totally set aside, save for your skills in asking good solution-focused questions.

It's about the team's solutions, no matter how confused or uncertain they may seem, or how much experience you have in their situation. Remember, your job is to help them find their expertise. Your expertise is helpful to them only in the quality of the better questions you ask.

2. Who's in charge of the thinking?

The team is in charge of thinking about what's troubling them and where they want to get to.

You are in charge of asking better questions, noticing what makes most sense (to the team), and overlooking what they say that doesn't help them make progress.

Occasionally, a team will have difficulty overcoming their Problem Focus. When this happens you may feel that you must try harder, that you're losing control. Remind yourself that the harder you try to make it work, the less it works for the team. Forget what you think about their problem. Start thinking about what better questions to ask that will move the team forward.

A wise Solution Focus trainer has said: "It's normal to get brown-outs when we are talking with our clients. They lead complex lives. What do you do? Just ask another Solution Focus question and give yourself some time to re-orient and think about a better question."

3. It's about their resources for their change

We have to remember that the person or team we are assisting has ample resources for change—change that's appropriate for them. It's just not yet visible to them. We cannot help them by applying our own ideas and resources (other than our better questions).

Think of yourself as a detective (in the chef's kitchen!). Through better questions the detective's job is to get the person or team to incriminate themselves—to produce evidence that proves they have already done something resourceful and useful. The Solution Focus detective is always looking for clues or evidence that the team has resources, that it knows what needs to change, and that it has ideas about how to make that change. The detective can help "incriminate" the team—show a weight of evidence that the team can make progress its way, right away!

4. Every case is different

Every individual is unique. So too, every team and every organization. They are composites of a vast amount of experiences, beliefs, and behaviors. Did you ever join a group or take up with a new partner only to find out something six months later that took you by surprise? No amount of sharing can reveal the whole picture.

The good news in Solution Focus is that *we don't have to know everything.* The less we know the better. The less we make assumptions about what's best for the team, the more help we can be. The more we remember that it's their experience and resources that matter, the more we can let them be resourceful themselves.

The saying "you can never step in the same river twice" also applies. When working with a team on subsequent occasions, remember that they will be different—because you helped them make progress last time. And a new team from an organization you've already worked with will certainly be different from the last one.

You might work with a group in a morning session, helping them make progress, then work with a similar group from the same organization in the afternoon who behave like they are from another planet.

Every case is different. Every interaction with every team is different.

5. Every solution is unique

If every case is different, so too every solution is different. This is another aspect of letting go. No matter that, to you, the solution is staring the team in the face, we must let go of the temptation to say or hint at something helpful. Even the best-meaning advice is unhelpful, particularly in the early stage of your interaction. The team may well agree with you, but in not letting them come to their own conclusions, they are less likely to embrace the change they need to make. Help them embrace the solution their way—the solution that is unique to their situation.

6. They are the experts, not you

The clients are the experts in the lives they lead, how they interact with others, and what they want to do. That's it.

They may not be very clear about, or good at, how they are doing it, but that's their choice, not yours. Your choice is to ask better questions about the expertise they have, no matter how obscure or difficult it is to bring to the surface. Your expertise is in the questions you ask.

Here's an example of how to help the team notice their expertise:

What would be most useful in our conversation today? (Helps focus their thinking on what they want to change.)

When does the problem not occur? (Helps them notice exceptions and the expertise they have.)

Suppose those exceptions to the problem happened more often in the future, what would you be doing instead? (Helps them apply their expertise.)

7. It's about making progress, not a revolution

Teams often put forward an abundance of reasons why the problem is very important and difficult to solve. So they look for a miracle solution in which everything is solved quickly. Occasionally, with our Solution Focus help they are ready for the miracle and they make a lot of progress right away. Mostly, they make great progress when they see the solution, but are not capable of making the entire change right away. This is especially true of teams. They can't all move quickly.

So, teams often look for a systemic change, not realizing the complexity of making that happen. Instead, Solution Focus can help them make situational changes. The future perfect or miracle question, (see #14, page 20) gives them an insight about what systemic change might work for them. From that starting point, the small-steps process can show them the steps to take toward that ideal. Does the future perfect have to ultimately happen? That's up to them, but it's not the issue. Having the small steps helps them see themselves making progress toward the future.

That said, it's important that the steps actually are small, and that they are concrete and doable.

8. The skeleton keys

Think of yourself and your questions as a set of skeleton keys (Steve DeShazer) that will open the door to the place the team wants to get to. Remember that the locksmith needs a bunch of keys; one skeleton key won't do it. So you are using questions to find out which key will unlock the team's doorway to change.

9. What's a better question?

Any question that helps the team move forward in their thinking is good. A question that keeps them focused on the problem isn't necessarily bad, but it will slow down their progress toward the solutions to which they aspire. It's easy to ask a question; it's a little more difficult to ask questions that are structured to help the team think differently.

Your job is to monitor the effect your questions have on them. Here are some examples of less effective questions (excursions) and good questions (direct routes).

Try this:

Direct route questions v. excursion questions (Shaun Lincoln* and Janine Waldman**)

Direct route questions (faster)	Excursion questions (slower)
How did you know how to do that?	Why did you do that?
What might you do differently?	What should you have done?
What have you done before that worked?	Have you done that before?
What did you do to contribute to the outcome?	Is there anything you did that helped?
What could you do to ensure this happens?	What are the obstacles to achieving this?
When have you been further up the scale?	Have you ever managed to do better?
How can you make sure this happens again?	Why can't you do that more often?
What else?	Anything else?
What did you learn from that?	Was that useful?
What small signs will tell you that you are on the right track?	What's stopping you?

How do we learn to ask the kinds of direct route questions on the left-hand side? Practice.

*Shaun Lincoln: shaunlincoln@hotmail.com
**Janine Waldman: janine@thesolutionsfocus.co.uk

10. What to expect when you ask a question

Don't expect anything. If we are anticipating the team's answers, we are setting ourselves up for a low-listening experience. Besides, their answers are going to surprise us anyway.

If the team's answer seems unhelpful and indicates that they are stuck in the same place, don't worry; they are on an excursion, thanks possibly to your excursion-like questions. (See Ingredient # 9, page 16, above)

11. Solution Focus language for setting a team up to succeed

The language we use is important. To illustrate the point review the following language.

Sample questions to get the team started:

- If you have a perfect day (meeting), what will be different?

- Suppose this conference has been really useful. It is now a year later; how are things now different in your work?

- How can you be useful to your fellow participants today?

- How will you have helped your organization to succeed?

- Thinking of [selected topic, such as "innovation"] in your organization, what has been going well for you lately?

- When your organization succeeds at [selected topic], how will the organization benefit?

- Suppose you and your organization make real progress. How will you have helped them achieve great things?

- At the end of the project, how will you have helped personally?

- If you were in the shoes of some of your staff, what concerns would they have for you? What would they like to see improved?

- What are the most positive outcomes for you in this new [selected topic] role?

- What are your grounds for optimism that your [selected topic] project will be a great success?

- Thinking of what's working, what would you want done differently?

- When you did something like this before, how did you make it happen?

- When you've hired people for new [selected topic] roles in the past, what worked?

- What three wishes do you have for your [selected topic] project?

- Tell yourself a story where something like [selected topic] didn't work and how you fixed it.

- Suppose that when you started the [selected topic] project it was a 3-out-of-10 and when you left it was a 9. What would you have done to make it work so well?

12. Showing them you are listening instead of thinking of answers to their issues

Solution Focus questions force us to listen. They are such interesting questions that we can't wait to hear the answers. However, you should resist the temptation to let the voices in your head get ahead of the team. There are many tools to show you are listening:

- Sit in a way that shows you are paying attention.

- Gently clench your teeth to avoid opening your mouth to say unnecessary words.

- Only open your mouth to:

  a) Ask a better question.

  b) Affirm some of the things the team is saying about their resources (see Ingredient #16, page 21).

- Ask questions that show how much you are listening—for example: "You said x and y. Suppose that were no longer happening; what would you be doing instead?"

13. Finding the resources already in place

The team actually does know what to do, but it's just not clear to them. Why? Because they have yet to fully notice the resources they already possess to make change happen. It's your job to be the detective who helps them see what those resources are. Sometimes the resources are abundant; other times you will have to help them dig deep to find them by seeking exceptions to the problem.

Seek to help the team by asking better questions about what they are already doing to deal with the change, or by asking about exceptions— times when the current problem was not happening.

By noticing these resources, the team can become hopeful that they will make progress and is more able to take on the miracle question (see Ingredient # 14 below).

Some sample questions that help resourcefulness to surface:

- What most pleases you about your work of late?

- You are obviously doing something right. What's that?

- List five examples where you have been resourceful in this area in the past.

- When the problem was not present, what did you and others (your clients, for example) notice you doing?

- Always add: How did you manage to do that?

14. The future perfect / the miracle question

Once they have insights about what's working (things they don't have to change), teams are able to be more hopeful about the future and what it will be like without the problem. Ask the future perfect / miracle question in order to get them to think of the possibilities.

Is the miracle question about the "right" or accurate picture of the future? No. Is it a place the team wants to get to? Yes.

The more detail the team can provide about the future—what they will be doing, the interrelationships of the key players and related stakeholders, the outcomes for the team (and others)—the clearer the alternative "truth" will be.

15. Yes, but is the difference sustainable?

It's up to the team!

We may wish them to have a revelation of the first magnitude and to change the rest of their lives. But they may decide to make a change that gets them to tomorrow (so they may be better able to handle tomorrow's issues).

We can help them decide how sustainable they want their efforts to be. Scaling (see Ingredient # 19, page 23), detailed resource descriptions, detailed imagery of the preferred future, and small first steps all help add to the potential sustainability.

16. Affirming and acknowledging

Affirmation and acknowledgement are powerful ways to help the team move forward. When a team recognizes they have a strength or an unconscious resource for change, they still might underestimate how important it is. It helps them if we acknowledge that: a) we were listening; b) it's worth noting. How we help them matters a great deal. However:

- Simply exclaiming "Fantastic!" every time they come up with something may be useful in the moment, but its resonance will wear thin.

- If we say, "Hmm!" too regularly, they will quickly stop noticing it.

- If we say, "I like how you described x, y, and z, and to me that's important, because you also said a while back that ..." and so on, we may be taking up the time they need to tell their version of the story.

So, what do we do? The answer lies within the team: we use a bit of everything based on where the team is in the moment of the interaction. If we want to encourage them to continue down a path they are finding useful, we might simply say, "That's interesting; tell me more," or "You seem pretty good at that." If they have just surfaced something they realize is important, a quick "Fantastic!" followed by, "How did you know how to do that?" helps them acknowledge themselves and learn more.

That said, there's the Wow! Factor (next).

17. The WOW! factor

Insoo Kim Berg seemed to use the affirmation "wow!" quite a lot, but her tone and delivery modulated greatly. One minute it could be a quiet wow; the next, almost an outburst. Her physical demeanor mattered a great deal; sometimes leaning forward, opening her eyes wide to say it. Other times, her chin in her hand, quietly letting the other person know she was engrossed in what they were saying.

All affirmations rely a lot on the tone of your language, your body stance, the point of inflection, and when you say it. Sometimes you can be quite theatrical. To a group who has just said something you recognize might be helpful to them, you might raise your arms and say:

"Wait a minute! A little while ago you said you were good at X, and now you are also saying you are good at Y! Wow! How did you manage to do that?"

Equally, you might simply and softly say, "Wow! That's great. What else?"

18. Lots of revelation through clarification

Letting the team talk about a problem—this may seem contrary to everything said before—is sometimes an important step for them to begin to move away from it. When they are defining and clarifying the difficulties, try to minimize talk about the cause of the problem. Causality is often the least productive conversation as it usually involves or leads to blame and creates further helplessness.

Clarification of the problem can be aided by helpfully restating the obvious:

"What I hear you saying is…" and purposefully overlooking the less useful parts, such as blaming.

Some gentle reframing also helps:

"I heard you saying X, and I also noticed that you did a good job managing that situation."

19. Helping them figure out where they are through scaling

Our Solution Focus questions can help us get a cursory view of where the team is in the moment. While our questions may be helping them notice things in a different way, the team may also be a bit disoriented or unsure of where to begin or where they have arrived. This is often an issue when working with a team—it only takes a few anxious people to make the rest of the group uncertain. They can't all be moving forward at the same time.

No matter. The scaling question is one of your (and their) best friends—a veritable Swiss-army knife of applications that help the team see where they are and where they'd like to get to.

It can also help a team find where they are collectively—at the beginning, middle, or end. When you ask a team, "If 1 is the not-so-good place and 10 is the ideal, where are you?" a variety of answers will emerge.

There are a host of possibilities—they may all be relatively close together, say from 5 to 8, or they may not, say from 2 to 7.
(See Paul Jackson's scaling recipe on Page 49)

20. Clarifying, affirming, and moving forward with scaling

No matter where they are on the scale, it's not your job to agree / disagree with their position. If the number seems unusually low or high to you, don't panic. It's where they are at that moment in time, and it's the right place for them.

Did they give a low number, such as 3? Slow down and dip into your toolbox of Solution Focus questions:

"Since you are at 3, what has helped you manage to get that far? What would it look like if you were slightly further up the scale? If the problem went away somehow, where would you be?" Note that focusing on the problems of why it's a 3 won't help.

If they are at 7, slow down and dip into your box of Solution Focus tools:

"What are you most pleased about, having arrived at 7? How have you arrived at 7? What small steps would it take to move you slightly up the scale? What would you see yourself doing to get there?"

21. There's no such thing as a bad Solution Focus question

If it's a Solution Focus question, you can do no harm.

There are less optimally structured Solution Focus questions. There are Solution Focus questions that create unintentional diversions (see #9, page 16/17, 'Excursions'). And if the team isn't making any progress, then you probably are not asking Solution Focus questions.

But any reasonably thoughtful Solution Focus question will help the team in some way, albeit tiny. It's the accumulation of the questions and answers that will help them make progress.

22. Take them seriously, not literally

People may say what seem to be mildly, or outrageously, frivolous things. Teams under pressure may say them regularly, especially as they have asked you to help them get unstuck from difficult situations. When they do, take them seriously. They mean it—in the moment, maybe even concretely.

You don't have to take what people say literally. Empathize, acknowledge, and accept that in the moment it's their reality.

Don't accept that it has to be dealt with right away. William James said, "The art of being wise is knowing what to overlook." In a Solution Focus context, things that don't make sense or aren't desired/helpful—anger, passivity, and so on—are best left unaddressed.

"We'll get back to that," works well.

23. Phrases and words to stop using

To be helpful to our clients it is purposeful to banish these types of words and phrases from our vocabulary:

You should…

You need to…

You can…

It would be better if you…

When we decide what the team "must" do, we weaken their efforts to find the solutions that will work for them. It is better that they create their own picture of where they have been, where they want to get to, and how to start going forward. Any effort to "tell" them starts to make it our picture. It will disrupt how they traverse the best route to change—a route only they can know.

24. Slowing things down to speed things up

Our Solution Focus dialogue with the team can occasionally lead to an excursion into the dialogue in which the team seems to be stuck. Or they simply get ahead of themselves. Burdened by anxiety about the size of the problem, they quite naturally let go of any spontaneous Solution Focus–based hopefulness and re-embrace helplessness. It's time to slow things down by suggesting something like, "Earlier we noticed that we have quite a lot working. Let's review the list." Or, "Sounds like you are a bit worried. Still, how do you see this conversation being useful to you so far?"

The team may have had a big insight about where they want to get to, but are intimidated by how much they think they have to do. When they say, "OK, we'll fix the IT system, develop new partnerships with customers, and bring in 500 new members," a voice in their heads is also saying, "Holy cow! How will we ever do that with the current mountain of projects?"

To alleviate their over-enthusiasm and unrealistic desire for systemic change, slow down the dialogue with questions like:

"Suppose we were to get there, but only took tiny steps in the early days; what are the micro-actions we would undertake? Who would do what? How would that be useful to you, your stakeholders, and so on? Where would you start? What would you do first? What's the main thing/issue that keeps you awake at night?"

25. Change as little as possible

As the team usually expects or feels that a lot needs to change in order to get unstuck, your drive to help them find their own small steps may seem at odds with their wishes. Remember that a lot does need to happen, but that's in their future perfect. We help them by noticing that they have resources (what's working) and that they do know what they want (future perfect). It's in the small steps that we help them move forward by changing as little as possible. This helps overcome self-imposed barriers to success based on fear of the amount of change required.

26. Learn a new language....Theirs

You won't need to go to school or buy a how-to book for this one. The place to learn the new language is with the team you're working with. Though you will talk in familiar terms, think of the team as being from another country that appears to speak the same language as yours. Not only will the dialect be different, the words will be too.

When a marketing manager sits down to talk with an IT manager, they will have their native language in common, plus the organization's language in common. The difference will be the language of their two practices. A marketing person might seem to work with fuzzy consumer concepts, while an IT person thinks in logical process-driven terms.

While they may have appeared to have a good conversation, there's a fair chance that the outcome—the work—will not be effective because certain concepts they think they understood were in fact misinterpreted. Only later do the unintended consequences become clear.

When we learn to hear what the team is actually saying, we can learn to understand what they said in their language. Still, there's always a temptation to show them what we think they are talking about, using our language. It's impolite. It won't help them to reveal what they actually want. They will see we are not fully listening to them. They will see that we did not understand what they were talking about, and they will be right.

27. Gently clench your teeth and listen

When people are stuck they often have trouble expressing themselves effectively. Given our human tendency to be helpful, we often want to support them by offering ideas or alternative views on the problem. Even if they agree with you, likely they still won't know what to do. Most often, our suggestions actually make little sense to them.

Instead, it suggests to them that we are not listening. And they are right. How can we ever know if our idea—blurted out in the moment—makes sense to their complex situation, most of which they don't have time to process and explain (usually because they are confounded/confused/mired in the problem)?

So, resist the temptation to calm them down with what seems to us to be obvious advice. To be helpful, we can visibly demonstrate that we are listening.

Try the affirmation technique #16, page 21. This will show them where you were listening.

Exceptions:

To help people move forward in the moment, it sometimes is helpful to say, "I wonder if you have considered..." Present this as mere curiosity on your part and remember that rejection of your question simply tells you that they need more help getting out of their complainant mindset. They may agree with your question, but then insist that it's someone else's job to fix the problem.

They may not be able to articulate what they want, yet unhelpfully to themselves, could prescribe what others need to do. The listener (you) is drawn into solutions that only work for the prescriber.

If so, go back and practice the technique above.

28. Helping them decide

Some teams and individuals make progress in a session but are still unsure what to do. Should we make a suggestion? No. They might like your ideas, but they won't be their ideas. Instead, you might ask, "Suppose you made progress on this issue, and your colleagues and your leader were congratulating you, what might they have seen you doing?"

Scaling where they are, followed by asking what a 0.5 move up the scale might look like, often opens them up.

29. When we work harder than the team

If we find that we are working harder than the team, it's likely that the session is also not working optimally for them.

When a team seems unwilling to move away from their problem it may be because they're not understanding our questions. And that's because we are not asking questions that make sense to them.

Better to slow down our expectations and start finding out what their needs are, what changes they want, and how they see things being different, if at all.

30. Yes, they do want your advice

Some say organizations are full of people dying to be told what to do, most often by their leaders. Some leaders understand this, while others don't see it that way. It's human nature. So, what you tell them matters. Yes, teams would like to be told the solutions to their problems, but not by us. We're not fully credible in their minds.

The exception: If we see the opportunity to give advice, it can be done as an offering.

"I wonder if you have ever considered or thought about trying..."

Its purpose can be solely to be helpful in moving them along. Its possible rejection by the team should be fully embraced by you. It's their decision. They're quite right to overlook our advice, if it isn't meaningful to where they are.

Any note of insistence such as, "You should consider..." changes the relationship right away. It undermines the idea of team as the expert and begins the process of "When I insist, you resist."

31. The more I insist, the more you resist

If you know parents who regularly lecture their children in strong terms, you'll know how little their children comply enthusiastically with the adults' wishes. If your manager told or lectured you to do something you didn't know how to do, or were unmotivated to perform, the chances of you ignoring or resisting are quite high.

So too with teams! We may notice something important that they need to do, but because we may only marginally know what's important to them there's a high chance the idea will fall in stony ground. At worst it will irritate them. To us it may be common sense. To them it shows we are not listening.

See Ingredient #24, page 25.

32. When the team can't stop complaining

Complainants are simply telling you they don't understand your questions. Don't assume that: a) they have not made any progress; b) they won't make progress (their way) at some point. Besides, some people like to hang on to their position even though they want to see things change. It's also common that complainants want other people to change first. The issue is to find out what they do want to change.

In teams, it may seem that the complainants are slowing down the others. Just remember that they are likely making progress - even though it may not be visible—their progress is what matters.

Slow down and dip back into the Solution Focus recipes with questions like:

"Suppose we had a conversation that was useful to you, what would need to happen? Again, it has to be helpful to you."

"If we were successful in addressing your needs, what would be the benefit to you?"

"What would you want to contribute to help the conversation?"

"When this happened before, what helped to make things better?"

"What resources do you have to deal with this sort of circumstance?"

"What do you want to achieve in this conversation?"

"How will you know that we have made some progress?"

"What makes you comfortable that we can make some progress in this session?"

"What else has been going well for you lately?"

33. When you, never mind they, are stuck

If you don't get stuck occasionally, you are either a genius or not able to notice that you are stuck. In helping the team peel back the complex layers of the situation, some of it will get fuzzy or daunting, particularly if they are not really interested in change.

The answer? Remember we said you can ask Solution Focus questions in any order that works for the team? When stuck, try any mildly useful Solution Focus question that occurs to you in the moment. It won't do the team any harm and it will give you time to think of a better question. Sometimes the randomness of the question will yield surprisingly good results.

34. Telling vs. coaching

In Solution Focus, the only telling we do is about the process, not about the team's content. A little mentoring can seem like an attractive approach to helping people: "I remember when I did that once and found that if I changed the way that I..." Though it may be helpful in the moment, and is sometimes sought by the team, it increases the risk of them not buying into the idea. For true buy-in, the team needs to create the ideas for themselves. Our system for change and our resources are attached to many factors that will not resonate with the team. You have to be patient in order to help them achieve their desired results or breakthroughs.

Coaching is about helping people find solutions that resonate for them. They are reframing what works for them—it's their system that they are leveraging for the changes they want.

Telling should be resisted no matter that the urge is only to be helpful.

Most of the human race is programmed to be helpful to each other. It's an instinct we have from childhood. So the powerful instinct in us to help teams is very strong. We all have a voice in us that says, "No, that's not what you should do. Here's what works." Worse still is the voice saying, "It won't work unless you do it this way..."

How do we overcome the instinct? By listening very intently and intensely, and by always checking with ourselves that we are asking Solution Focus questions that work for the team.

Again, slow down. Remember that the best thing Solution Focus can do to help the team is change as little as possible—their way.

Coaching and mentoring can seem similar. The critical difference is in expectations of the word "mentor"—that the mentor brings their experiences, shares their point of view, suggests actions, and so on. The coach rarely shares their perspective in favor of letting the team work out things for themselves.

A coach can use mentoring skills, but will more often enable the team to work out things for themselves.

35. When to go out on a limb

Can you go out on a limb with a little "telling"? Very rarely. Very carefully.

The line "rejection often offends" should be remembered when the team gets confused or, more likely, ignores your ideas. If the problem they face re-occurs they may blame you!

36. A beginning, a middle, and an end

Team interventions in particular seem to have greater impact and sustainability for the team when there is a beginning (sometimes pre-work), a middle (the intervention they asked for), and an end (follow-through: "what's different?").

37. Situations where you might apply the Solution Focus tools and recipes

Every team and every situation is unique. Solution Focus is built on the principle that as everyone has a unique view of their life, the work we do should be infinitely variable (determined by the team's requirements). In organizations much of the work is about reducing variables, usually in order to create predictable outcomes.

A better meeting

Planning

Aligning a team around a difficult decision they have to make

Aligning cross-functional teams that have discrete (conflicting) goals

Assessing what to do when:

- a significant problem has arisen

- morale and motivation is low

- performance reviews are happening

- a new target has been set

- the team needs to align with outside stakeholders

- two individuals are at odds

- staff and management are in different places (not geographically)

- a merger happens

- a team feels it is powerless to influence others

- a team feels is not getting cooperation from others

- a group needs to learn new skills and demonstrate they can deliver

- a team is negative and prone to gossip and complaining

- a team is capable, but stuck

- a team is low on capabilities, and stuck

- a team wants to assess their performance

- a team wants to influence others over whom they have no authority

- a team wants to enhance its performance and efficiency

- a team is powerful and wants others to be as successful

- two systems don't fit together

- a team is trying to persuade management to change its mind

- teams seem to be at war with each other

- a team doesn't recognize the importance of goals and outcomes for the customer

- a team has determined its own goals and appears to be intransigent

- change has to happen fast

- individuals resist change

- leadership is not clear in its goals and the team still has to make things happen

- a team has to learn to deal with ongoing unpredictability

- the culture has to change

- process tools (like change) are in place but they don't seem to be working

- there's no clear plan and things need to happen

III. THE SOLUTION FOCUS RECIPES

Here are some proven recipes for speeding up progress. They are contributions from a variety of Solution Focused practitioners who have been using the approach for many years. A big thank you goes to the contributors who ask you to use the ideas, but to not forget to refer source!

Andry Anastasiou - Helen Bailey - Kirsten Dierolf - Paul Z Jackson
Björn Johansson - Carey Glass - Michael Klingenstierna Hjerth
Jackie Keddy - Shaun Lincoln - Guenter Lueger
Dr Mark McKergow - Coert Visser

There are two categories of recipes:

1. Recipes for **everyday** interventions (snacks)

2. Recipes for **larger scale** interventions or significant parts thereof (main meals)

1. Recipes for everyday interventions:

a) Setting the scene (Shaun Lincoln*)

Scenario:

Unexpected meeting with someone at a conference

When to use:

When you have limited time in which to influence someone and make your proposal and get them interested or on board.

Why use:

Reduce the actual time needed to make your point, stay focused and increase the likelihood of a follow up meeting.

*Shaun Lincoln: shaunlincoln@hotmail.com

On the spot influencing tool

1. How much of an issue is <insert topic> for you at the moment?

2. What is the most important thing that needs to be done?

3. Suppose you could make progress on that, what would be the benefits?

4. What else would be beneficial?

5. I have some ideas about <insert topic>. Would you be interested?

6. <Make your proposition>

b) Preparing for 1:1s - to help your staff maintain or improve performance (Shaun Lincoln* & Helen Bailey*)

B asks A

What do you want to achieve from the 1:1? How will that benefit you?

What else do you want to achieve from the 1:1? How will that benefit you?

What might the other person want to achieve from the 1:1?

How will that benefit them? What else might they want from the 1:1? How will that benefit them?

What is this person doing that you like and want more of?

What tells you that? Do they know this?

What one thing do you want them to do differently as a result of the 1:1? How can you best support them to achieve this?

Suppose someone who knows them really well were here right now, what advice would they give you?

*Shaun Lincoln: shaunlincoln@hotmail.com   **Helen Bailey: Pinna, Helen@pina.co.uk

Debrief: Preparing for 1:1s

What worked? What did you notice?

Where could this tool be useful?

How does it help with understanding what motivates and engages individuals?

How does it help with autonomy, mastery and purpose?

c) Catch them doing something right (Andry Anastasiou*)

What valuable/ fantastic/ positive/creative* things you have done recently that I have noticed *Add in the employees or organizational *value*	Positive impact you have had on the team/ the organization (choose a point that links to a team goal or organizational strategy)
Places I have seen you take the initiative /without even being asked (choose a point that links to a team goal or organizational strategy or to the persons' last supervision or appraisal)	What (possible) opportunities all of this is opening up for you in your job/ role (link this to what you know about the employee's goals and/or team and organizational vision or to appraisal)

*Andry Anastasiou, Team Training andry@teamtraining.org.uk

d. Capturing success (Andry Anastasiou*)

How often at the end of project do we rush onto the next project ...
...without acknowledging and celebrating success?

Capturing success

Working in pairs decide who is A and B

A invites B to think of a project or significant piece of work they have achieved with others and to describe it briefly.

Questions for A

What impressed you most about your staff/ colleagues during this piece of work? (what else?)

What did others say that pleased you about this piece of work? (What else?)

Of all the things that went well what would you do more of in future? (What else?)

What might you do differently next time?

e) Just a Minute Micro tool (Jackie Keddy**)

Scenario:

You are pushed for time and one of your team comes up and says, 'have you just got a minute...?'

When to use

When busy, under pressure to meet a deadline or with 5 minutes to go before a briefing/meeting, when leaving a meeting. In the corridor, anywhere

*Andry Anastasiou, Team Training andry@teamtraining.org.uk
**Jackie Keddy www.keddyconsultants.com

Why use

5 minutes will save hours or days later.

The questions:

- How urgent is it?

- What's the problem?

- Where are you with that? What have you done to now?

- Where would you like to be?

- What's working well?

- Tell what you are impressed with/ give recognition

- What do you need to do now?

- What will be the first small steps you will take?

- What else?

f) Pre Meeting tool (Michael Klingenstierna Hjerth*)

Scenario:

Meetings are where minutes are taken and hours wasted

When to use

When busy, 5 minutes before a meeting, to ensure you or the other person/people make best use of it

*Adapted from Hjerth. michael@solutionwork.se

Why use

Reduce the actual time needed in the meeting, increase the likelihood of useful actions coming out as a result.

The questions:

1. What is the purpose of the meeting?

2. What result would you like to see?

3. What has worked previously (to do this)?

4. What can you do now?

5. What else?

6. What needs to come first?

g) Day Planner Tool (Michael Klingenstierna Hjerth*)

Scenario:

We can not manage time, but we can manage ourselves

When to use

At the beginning of the day, every day, 3 minutes before you turn on the mail or mobile

Why use

3 minutes spent using this tool can save hours later, and help ensure you make best use of your time and that of others and that the day is effective. Typically saves 20% of your time, better time management, better results.

*Adapted from Hjerth. michael@solutionwork.se

Ensure you manage your day as it progresses

1. Where will I concentrate on today?

2. What MUST I do today?

3. How can I make this easier for myself?

4. What needs to come first?

5. What next?

6. What events might prevent me from doing this?

7. How can I best anticipate these?

8. What else?

h) Team Interview Technique (Björn Johansson*)

A asks B, then B asks C, then C asks A (one question at at time)

- Of all the things you're doing at work at the moment, what would you say you are MOST pleased with?

- Of all the OTHER things you're doing at work at the moment, what would you say you are most pleased with?

- In view of that, and all the other good things you are doing, what would be most interesting for you to develop over the next few weeks on this program?

- What will be the first signs that tell you that you have gone one step further in what you want to develop?

*Björn Johansson, www.clues.se

i) Every client is different: Visitors Complainers and Customers (Coert Visser*)

Here Coert Visser provides a handy tool for appraising three typical types of participants; Visitors, Complainers and Customers.

Interaction	Meaning	Some example interventions
Visitor-typical	The client does not (yet) see the usefulness of tire conversation	• Explore/clarify reason for having the conversation • Explore the perspective of the client • Ask the usefulness question • Summarizing in the words of the client
Complainer-typical	The client sees the usefulness of the conversation but behaves helpless and complains. The client does not see how he may be part of the problem and of the solution.	• Accept and acknowledge the perspective of the client and work with that • Normalizing • Reframing • Further explore how the conversation may become useful for the client • How does the client want his situation to become?

*Coert Visser: www.m-cc.nl

Customer-typical	The client sees the usefulness of the conversation, welcomes help and is prepared to take steps to improve his situation	• Desired situation question • Scaling question • Platform question • Past success question / Exception seeking questions • Step forward question • Usefulness question

j) Making the most of the team's existing change resources (author)

Every briefing from a team should be met with the request: "When you tackled this sort of change / planning in the past, what worked?" This gives you an insight into the way they like to work. (Another good question: "When you worked with a consultant / coach in the past, what worked?")

Some of the tools they previously found useful may need to be "enhanced" because, though helpful, they are often problem-focused. Here's an example—the tested and true SWOT analysis beloved of banks and the like.

2. Recipes for a full intervention, or significant parts thereof

a) A recipe for Solution Focused 360 Feedback (Kirsten Dierolf*)

Today many companies use 360 degree feedback systems to help their managers and leaders to develop. Most often these systems consist of predetermined questions around the leadership values that the organization has identified as part of a strategic leadership culture initiative. These questions are then put into an online system. Each leader in the organization can then send this questionnaire to informants of their choice: their bosses, their peers, their direct reports or even customers. Each of the informants answers the questions by checking a box between "agree completely" and "disagree". In most systems there is even room for one or two verbal comments. What I found working with these systems is that most managers immediately go to the verbal comments and ignore the average numbers and the range. And, indeed, it is very hard to say what exactly it means when somebody slightly disagrees with the statement "Mr. Y is a visionary leader". It is actually even harder for the recipient of the 360 degrees feedback to find out what to do to become a more visionary leader or even to know whether this is what people want from him. Open Space Technology resulted from the observation that "the most important conversations happen in the coffee break". My SF 360 Feedback is derived from a similar observation: "Talking about solutions helps". So whenever you would like to help an organization create better leaders in their company, SF 360 Feedback is a good option to choose.

How it works:

First step:

You have an individual meeting with the leader who would like to get better at what she does. The conversation is mainly a goal setting conversation. You ask questions like:

- If this 360 degrees feedback process is useful for you what will be different afterwards?

- On a scale of 0-10, where are you now with regard to these goals? (or several scales)

- What tells you it is already at X and not at 0?

45

- What could be a next step that you know about already?

- What would you like to know about how others perceive you? What are you curious about?

- Who would be good people to call? (In my experience it is good to encourage the reader to be bold and look for a good mix of people who they get along with well and people who are more critical. It is also good to get the feedback of the direct superior.)

Second step:

You ask the leader to politely ask for 15 minutes of each informant's time and supply you with a list of phone numbers and e-mail addresses of the people you should call. Set up appointments for telephone conversations with each of the informants. On a practical level it makes sense to do these calls from your computer with a headset phone so you can type while the informants are giving their answers. If you are not a quick typer, you can also record the conversations, but then he will obviously need the informant's permissions. I have very good experience with quickly typing the main points of each informant and then rereading what I wrote down to them. It seems like the fact that I use the informants' language in my summaries built a lot of trust in me and the process.

Third step:

When you are having the phone conversations with the individual informants, introduce yourself, quickly explain that the conversation is confidential and that you will only supply an anonymized report to the leader XY and that she will not know who said what.

In the phone conversations you can ask questions like:

- On a scale of 0-10, where 10 is optimal collaboration and 0 the opposite – where are you now?

- What does leader XY do to make it possible that it is not 0?

- What should leader XY definitely continue doing?

- What would X+1 look like? How would you notice that leader XY is moving up a step?

- What is some of your well-intentioned advice for leader XY?

- Is there anything that I forgot to ask but that is important for leader XY to know?

- While the informants are answering, your write down the relevant information. When an informant is very general, e.g. "leader XY is not visionary enough", you persistently ask for concrete information: "how would you notice that she is more visionary?" or "what would be the first tiny sign that she is becoming more visionary"

Fourth step:

You find a way to communicate the gathered information to the recipient of the 360 degrees feedback. I usually write a report in which I summarize what people said and take care to include those things that leaders should continue doing and concrete ideas for what leader might change to become even more effective. We then work on the identified topics in coaching sessions – usually not many coaching sessions are necessary because the leader has a lot of concrete suggestions that she can try out just by reading the report. Most often there are 2 more sessions in about 6 weeks time.

Effects:

When you compare the SF 360 Feedback with the usual online 360 degrees products, the SF 360 Feedback compares favorably:

Traditional 360 Feedback computer based	SF 360 Feedback
Expensive setup of the questionnaire	No set-up cost – cheap pilot sessions are possible.
15 minutes per informant necessary to fill in partially irrelevant questions (not all questions will be applicable for everyone)	15 minutes per informant necessary – only relevant information is elicited
Sometimes low quality of the answers	High quality answers are ensured
Sometime not apparent what to do with the answers	Answers provide meaningful suggestions
Individual strengths are considered only in a generalized way	Individual strengths and good behaviors are recognized and strengthened
Little positive influence of answering the questionnaire on the informants (except, maybe, reinforcement of the company values in a very general way)	Providing a paradigm for giving feedback and continuing improvement based on individual strengths and improvement possibilities. People find out how to talk about it when they need someone to change something – and also find out how good it is to mention the positive points

Extension:

If you work with several coaches in the same organization it makes sense to provide the company with the opportunity to listen to a "resource gossip" and "reflecting team" where the coaches sit together and talk about what goes well in the company and what they have heard that might benefit from some attention. While the coaches are talking, the leaders of the organization listen and then talk about what they have heard and what they want to keep doing and what they would like to try doing a bit differently as a group.

*Kirsten Dierolf, SolutionsAcademy, Germany kirsten@solutionsacademy.com

b) The Scaling Walk (Paul Z Jackson*)

An important part of any cooking experience is pacing up and down while the mixtures heat up and transform themselves into a delicious meal. The skilled facilitator makes good use of this time – perhaps using a Scaling Walk, as described here.

This is an active and engaging way to enable all your participants/guests to address an issue of importance – such as raising their performance in an aspect of work.

It takes about 10 minutes to run, and another 10 to debrief. You can use it with any number of people. The only limit is the width of the room or space you are using.

Let your group know that the purpose of this activity is to offer each one of them a powerful insight into raising performance. And we're going to walk the scale.

Directions

Either create a space big enough in the room or take the participants outside or to a more suitable room.

Then ask everyone to focus their minds on the issue that has brought them together, and to choose one aspect of that topic at which they would like or need to improve. Check that everyone has something to work with.

Tell them, "Ten represents you performing consistently at your personal peak, in your chosen activity - the best you can be. One is you stuck at the worst you imagine it can be for you. Where on that scale are you now?"

"So we can work together, let's call that number (whatever it is) 'n'."

Ask them to keep the number to themselves.

What's at 10?

*Paul Z Jackson, www.thesolutionsfocus.co.uk paul@thesolutionsfocus.co.uk

Let them know that that there is now a scale in the room, and show them which end is 1 and which is 10. Ask the participants to join you, standing up at a point about half way along the scale (the middle of the room), that you designate as 'n'.

When they are on the line, ask them if they would rather face 1 or 10 … most participants prefer to face 10.

Ask them all to face 10 and then ask them what is appealing about facing this way as opposed to 1. Get a few answers: these might range from fantastic to scary. You can point out that different people view 10 differently. They don't need to identify the aspect of the topic that they are working on – just their attitude. An alternative is to make all the questions in this activity rhetorical and have only the facilitator speak.

Now ask them, "What does being on a scale imply?" The crucial answer is that being on a scale implies the possibility of movement to a different point on that scale – that it implies the possibility of progress (or regress, for that matter). The idea of movement is built into the idea of a scale. Scales presuppose movement. Simply by placing yourself on a Scale, you have implications of potential movement - and therefore possible progress.

Avoiding problem talk about the topic

Ask what comes to mind when they turn to look at 1. They may say "failure, depressed, hard work". Listen for someone saying "learning, resources etc" or introduce the idea by saying something along the lines of, "I'm guessing that to get to where you are on the scale, you've done some impressive things, learned a lot, overcome obstacles and had successes. Maybe this space between 'n' and 1 represents that learning…or a sea of know-how and counters that's got you to where you are."

You can explain that we are not going to visit 1 on the scale, and ask the group why that might be. "What's significant about 1?", "What do we need to know about 1?","How much detail do we need to have of what 1 looks/feels like?". The answer is that 1 represents Problem Talk, and that facilitators (and perhaps they as managers) generally find it a lot less useful to focus on problem talk than solution talk.

Ask them to take a moment to appreciate all the skills, knowledge, successes etc, that make up that sea of know-how, maybe even to give themselves a pat on the back.

Now walk the entire Group along to 10 on the scale, the other end of the room. Ask them to visualize 10, closing their eyes if they find it easier. "What is it like? What are they doing that tells them they are at 10? What do others notice? What can they see? What is being said? How does it feel? What is happening?"

Ask "Who has been at 10, for real, for a period, a moment … (That's the source of useful know-how too)."

Give them a moment to visualize 10, then ask them to open their eyes and ask for two or three volunteers to share their experiences of 10. Again here it is useful to notice, if relevant, people's different experiences and expectations of 10.

Ask "What does 10 represent?" "How much detail do we want about 10?" "What's the point of mentally visiting 10 on the scale?"

Small steps

Invite participants to now come back to n…and ask them what's different now about looking to 10. (Often people say they feel inspired, motivated, they know something they didn't know before).

Ask if they can go straight to 10 from where they are now. If they could, then as a facilitator you would invite them to do so. If not, what might they be able to do now instead. The answer is to make a small step – one point up the scale. And we can do this by looking at the know-how we've used to get to n, including what we've learned about 10.

Then ask them to close their eyes, for them to notice what would be the first sign that would tell them that they have moved up the scale, say half or one point. What would they be doing, seeing etc? Then invite them to think of a small step they could take in the following days/weeks that would move them up the scale, and when they have thought of the step to physically take a step forward…..then to open their eyes…and notice that 10 is nearer.

Invite them to turn around again, and ask what is in the space between 'n' and where they are now. The answer is fresh know-how, recent momentum that might help them make further progress.

Surprises

Ask the group to return to their seats, ask any questions and make any notes that will be useful.

As you can tell, I like to make learning concrete and experiential. Walking the scale seemed one way to achieve this with the concept of solution-focused scaling. I introduced it at an EBTA conference workshop, and have developed it in almost every solutions-focused training since then.

People often say they appreciate the physicality of the activity and many say they experience a profound visualization – especially at 10. It was surprising when some participants said they now realized they didn't want to be at 10. You can ask them then what number they would like to be at.

c) The MOP scale: When there are Multiple Organizational Projects (Björn Johansson*)

The MOP – scale (Multiple Organizational Projects)

Set up a platform

- What are the different projects? Formulate them into action. (Something you do, are up to that you want to develop. Eg get better meetings, develop collaboration, etc)

- Build groups around each project. 2-6 persons who have the project in common. 20 persons can for example work with 5-6 different projects.

- Make sure that the project is an urgent task and that the group can see themselves as a "part" in the project.

- Clarify frames and conditions if this is unclear to some of the group members.

Usually most of this is quite clear from the beginning, which means that you have set up the platform right. Invite their skills in working disciplined and structured.

*Björn Johansson, www.clues.se

A/ What do you want to reach?

Pretend you all sitting here X months from now and this project you have worked with has developed surprisingly well. In some way you have made all these advantages that have changed the situation in the way you wanted. It is (for example +5 months) and things are working really well in order to the conditions you have had…

Instruction: Just think, don't answer, and only write some keywords down.

What signs are telling you that you have reached what you want?

What else?

In what way is it different?

What are you doing different as a result of that?

(In some projects you can use questions related to the third person. – What will your costumer, boss, clients see you do different… or how will they know that you have made progress)

Instruction: Discuss in each group what you are doing different in the scenario ex month from now, how it looks like. Not what you will DO to GET there. These ideas will come later on. One person in each group takes notes and get the role of a coordinator if necessary.

5-7 minutes.

B/ Scaling

On a scale from 0 to 10, where 10 stands for; the project has developed just the way you just talked about. 0 stands for; you do not do anything of what you just talked about.

Where would you say you are right now? Every group's average. 2 minutes.

C/ What are you doing already?

What of the things you are doing at 10, are you doing already?

Find out as many things you can think of. List them and be concrete.

6-8 minutes.

D/ What can you do more of?

Divide the answers in C between you in pairs. What of this can you do more of in the next coming weeks (max 4), to make progress on the scale?

Write down your ideas and formulate them into action.

Too may ideas? Prioritize them. 6-8 minutes.

E/ Reflecting – Adding

Every group present their ideas very briefly. Other groups listen carefully and gives feedback, reflect and may add to their ideas. Time depends of the number of groups. If the participants in each group got nothing to do with other groups project and you have a limited time, you can choose to jump over this phase.

F/ Is it enough?

Every group consider if they have enough of ideas to go on with in the present day situation? 2 minutes.

If not; what else do they have to do?

G/ Action plan

Make an action plan involving who, when, what etc. rather less than covering too much. Give priority to ideas if necessary. Make sure that you are convinced that you can do what you planned. Good luck!

d) The Solution Focused Performance Appraisal (Carey Glass* & Guenter Lueger**)

The following is brief extract from the book; The Next Generation of Performance Appraisal by Carey Glass and Guenter Lueger. It will shift the way performance appraisal system are used to dramatically change measurement, conversations and outcomes.

The Trap of Performance Appraisal

Have you ever had a difficult discussion in a performance appraisal? As a manager have you gone in with the best of intentions to find yourself ending up in a debate? As an employee have you felt that the ratings have been unfair and the discussion demoralizing?

Most performance appraisal systems have one thing in common; you are asked to place your employee or yourself in a category on a scale. You might have a range of words like poor, average, good and excellent or numbers from 1 for the worst performance, through to 5 for the best. Whatever the system, you need to choose a specific point for every skill or competence that your system measures.

We've all been trained to work this way. But it is actually this very familiar act of choosing a point on a scale that traps you into many of the sticky problems you get caught with during performance appraisals.

This trap is based on a fallacy that is built into the system; the assumption that the level of our performance is always the same, when in fact our performance varies.

*Carey Glass www.thehumancentre.co.uk
**Guenter Lueger www.solutionmanagement.at

Customer Service

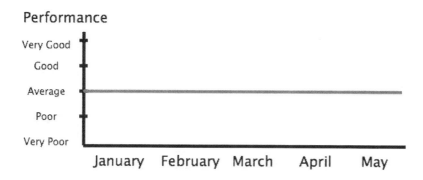

In a performance appraisal, you may be asked to rate someone's customer service for the last six or twelve months, The system forces you to choose one point on the scale. When displayed on a graph you can see that you are being forced to describe their performance as consistent on that particular point throughout the time period.

Now look at the graph below.*

Customer Service

Discuss and learn from above the line

If necessary, apply to below line to find small steps

*Graphic courtesy of Mark McKergow.

It is no wonder therefore when you are in a performance appraisal conversation that things go awry despite the best intentions of both parties. The system does not allow you to track reality. If you have described an individual's performance as average, they are justifiably going to describe examples of their best performance and you are either going to give in or remind them of that delivery they forgot to arrange. The system can only serve to sour the outcome.

What can we do to make progress on this issue?
Solution Focus Review (SFR) and The Advantages Of Doing It Differently

- SFR Reduces Conflict

- SFR Transforms Conversations

- SFR Creates a Positive Mindset

- SFR Recognizes That People Have The Answers Within Them

- With SFR Development Objectives Become Clear

- With SFR Steps To Goal Achievement Are Easily Mapped Out.

- With SFR Context Is Taken Into Account

- SFR Decrease The Blame Cycle

- With SFR You Can Be An Appreciative Rather Than A "Neutral" Manager

- With SFR Performance Appraisal Finally Matches A Changing World.

Now have your first go at doing an appraisal differently.

Start by having the person appraise your own performance. Have them bring to mind examples of their performance on that competence and record the variation in your performance by distributing 100 percentage points along the scale below.

Solution Focused Rating

Reviewee: self assessment
- Think about your performance at work over the past year.
- Award yourself 100 points spread over these categories:

Poor	OK	Good	Fantastic!

Reviewer: interview the reviewee
- Now, work with the reviewee's assessment as the basis for a performance discussion, using SF ideas:
- Start from the top end 'Fantastic!': When was this, what about it made it fantastic, elicit strength, skills etc, how could this category be made even bigger next year.
- Then move on to 'Good' and repeat, and so on till time is up.

Now have the individual answer questions in the order 1 – 10 below. Start completing details on the right column – what would your customers, colleagues etc., tell me about what you do is fantastic, good, etc:

Solution Focused **Future** Performance

Scope for improvement	OK	Good	Fantastic!
4.	3.	2.	1.

7. Suppose #4 above were no longer an issue in the future. What would you be doing instead?

5. What would others say is the essence of your success (#1–2)?

6. Suppose more of #1–2 happened in the future. What would be even better?

8. What first small steps might you take to make progress right away?

Concept adapted from Gunter Lueger & SFWork

e) Turning the corner from problem to solution: (Dr Mark McKergow*)

Title and subtitle of the activity:

What do we have to get right?

Turning the corner from problem to solution

Short description:

Sometimes people seem to love to talk about problems. This exercise allows them to do so, while staying solution focused.

Frame:

- This activity can take from 15 – 30 minutes, depending on the context. There are many variants which can take more or less time.

- This activity works well for any number of people from one upwards.

Uses:

This is an excellent activity to get things moving in a workshop. Having set up a good solid platform, this activity can add a lot of detail to the solution whilst giving people the chance to raise the issues as they see them.

Purpose and practical effect:

In workshops and team coaching sessions, participants often want to talk about what's wrong. Shutting this discussion down too quickly can lead to people feeling they are not being taken seriously. However, leading the group into a discussion of what they must get right in moving forwards lets them discuss issues and at the same time turn from 'what's wrong' to 'what do we want' – the crucial distinction between problem and solution.

*Dr Mark McKergow PhD MBA, United Kingdom www.sfwork.com

Detailed description:

There are many ways to use this basic idea. This is one format I use with teams, following the classic think-pair-share sequence.

Having established a good working atmosphere and established the issues the team wants to work on, I make sure that everyone has a pen and paper and announce:

Next, we're going to think about the issues relating to this topic. I would like each of you to take a few moments to think quietly about this question. 'What do we have to get right in moving forward with this? Write down as long a list as you can of the things we must get right. Three minutes. Go.

Everyone thinks hard and writes fast – some lists will be longer than others, that's OK. Then I ask people to pair up – possibly with the person next to them, or by some other means. If there are people from different departments or levels, I might ask groups from the same department or level to work together. I give them five minutes to discuss their lists and combine them, and start to prioritize the items. The time for this phase is extendable, of course, if the discussion seems particularly productive.

I then start to gather the items by going around each group and getting an item from the top of their priority list. I write the item on a flip chart, taking great care that the words match what was said. If an issue is presented as a problem, I can turn it around by saying something like:

Yes, that's an important issue. So, what do we have to get right in relation to this?

Move fairly quickly around the groups so that everyone gets a turn. I like to get all the items onto the list if possible, so that no-one thinks that anything has been ignored. The flip chart is then displayed on the wall.

Once that has been done, it's usually time to move to a Future Perfect activity or some such. This can be framed as being what happens if, suppose we were indeed to get all these things right. It adds a lot of potential detail to the next steps, as well as kick-starting thinking about 'life with the problem vanished' – the solution in solution-focus.

The "Knack" - Background and comments:

- I developed this activity during a team workshop. The team wanted to discuss the 'hot topics' facing them in relation to a reorganization. I rephrased the question, and it turned out to be very effective, getting lots of ideas into view as well as being a great basis to develop a Future Perfect.

- I think it's important that people don't feel pushed from problem to solution. If they come up with problem-talk I think to myself that it's not that they have got the activity wrong – it's just that they have not finished it yet.

- The level of the answers does not need to be specific – the specifics are usually generated in the next stage. So, if people say that communication between the managers and the team has not been good, and therefore communication needs to be better, that's fine. Going into more detail (as we might do in a Future Perfect or Counters exercise) may lead to disagreements about the nature of the better communication – not usually what's wanted at this stage. This is a part of building the platform.

Technical requirements:

Pens and paper, flip chart

What happens next:

I would strongly suggest a Future Perfect activity. This allows all the factors identified in this exercise to be combined together into a working description, leaving behind the individual issues.

Finding words:

- Before the workshop

- Focal points

- Activities in the beginning

Problems; issues; hot topics; platform

f) A strategic-planning team-input session (author)

Here's how to make a planning session yield a good deal of organizational alignment by facilitating a better dialogue about strategic matters. This is an opportunity to use Solution Focus from the beginning of the team's planning period and help them see a difference right away. The difference will be in having the planning team and other stakeholders create solutions and notice the change happening right away.

You may or may not help write the planning document. Teams who write the planning document often feel more accountable for its implementation.

Plan for facilitating a strategic (or operational) planning project

Steps:

1. The organization's current plan.

   - Team reviews the plan. You ask: "What worked? What needs to be different?"

2. Ask: "In thinking of the key challenges / opportunities we face, what are the four to five most useful questions we need to answer in the planning work?"

   - Avoid "boiling the ocean." Use best judgment in setting the questions.

3. Team develops four to five answers using the Key Question / Opportunity format (next page).

   - Teams formed to answer the questions (one per team).

   - Teams utilize research, existing knowledge, but not a lot of in-depth study, just their best thinking.

4. Conduct a team planning session to review the answers and develop a picture of what is wanted in the future.

   - Teams present Key Question / Opportunity one at a time.

- Larger group are asked to discuss:
  Suppose this were to be achieved in x years, what would be happening?

- (There are no "right" answers, just helpful assumptions about what we want to happen in the future.)

- Split group into teams that each answer from a different stakeholder perspective.

- Have "answer" written on flip charts and have groups share their thinking.

- Once all the key questions have been addressed, have the group create a list of strategic priorities.

- Have the groups develop strategies for each priority.

- Discuss any small-step actions that can take place while the plan is being documented by management.

5. Client develops / writes the plan.

- Match the existing organizational format or create a new one.

6. Conduct a follow-through meeting in which the key question is: 'What's different since the planning session?'

Sample Key Question Format:

<u>Planning Period 20XX–XX</u>

<u>Key Planning Question</u>

<u>Insights & Opportunity</u>

Key Question / Opportunity, for example: "The organization must strive for excellence in customer focus. How will we achieve that?"
(response goes here)

Market observation:
(response goes here)

Key insight:
(response goes here)

A vision of where we need to get to on this topic over the next three years. Imagine it is 20XX (end of planning period). Based on the above insight, what are we doing well in this area? For example: "We are the first-choice provider of…" Describe the picture in some detail.
(response goes here)

It's 20XX. How is that useful and of value to our customers? What are they now doing?
(response goes here)

Looking back at [current year], what were some of the strategies we undertook to get started?
(response goes here)

g) Making the change sustainable and noticeable—a follow-through discussion (author)

Workshop participants will typically commit to make visible change happen quickly. They often make immediate progress and the resulting change has an impact on the project as a whole—situational change contributes to systemic change. This progress can sometimes be made less visible by other projects and ongoing work. The opportunity exists to help the team make the progress and sustainability easier to see. Here's one way to help them amplify their successes and encourage them to take on even more change (in other words, convert their progress from situational to systemic).

Purpose

Maintain and build change sustainability by helping teams and individuals raise consciousness of the amount of progress they have made.

- Look at what has worked well (including what's worked moderately well and, perhaps, not at all well).

- Notice how it has made a difference.

- Help reinforce the growth and changes that have happened and encourage the team to make even more progress.

Format

Follow-through discussion meeting.
One to two hours, usually four to six weeks after the workshop.
Comprising: six to eight project / workshop participants.
Example discussion outline:

1. Thinking of the activities in your area, what's different since the [event]?

2. What were the best things you did afterward?

3. What would customers say were the best things you did?

4. How did you do those things?

5. What did you learn from doing those things?

6. How was the session / workshop we did together useful to you?

7. What will you now do more of or do differently?

8. What is the next task in front of you?

9. What will that look like when you have achieved it?

h) Team small-steps action planning (author)

When a team has realized where they want to get to and have developed small steps to get there, it's helpful to them if they commit their thinking to paper. The purpose is not to create a checklist for their manager, but a learning tool about what to do, and the implications of doing it. Think of it as a micro–miracle question.

Action Planning for Simple and Visible initiatives

Based on our view of the future and building on our existing skills choose a small project that your team can implement in the next 1 – 2 weeks. Customers will see or feel a difference with the implementation of this project.

Things to think about:

1. You and your team are the resource for change and growth
2. Include any groups and/or activities and whether you need to communicate your plans with others.
3. Think about how you will notice progress.

1. Our goal and what it will look like when our team has accomplished it?	**4. With whom do we see ourselves collaborating and communicating to help make this happen?**
2. How do we see this helping with the unique needs of our customers?	**5. When? What time frame for the actions will we have set up?**
3. Where will we begin? What will be the first visible steps? **A.** **B.** **C.**	**6. How will we be communicating our successes?**

Alan Kay: The Glasgow Group www.glasgrp.com

i) A post-session evaluation (author)

Session evaluations have a habit of superficially quantifying the participants' likes and dislikes of the process. They don't reveal much for the participants. A solution-focused evaluation form helps the participant revisit what they learned, reflect on the impact their learning will have, and consider what they plan to do themselves. The measurement-based component can be tabulated for comparisons with other team sessions.

Workshop
Session Evaluation Form

1. **On a scale of 1 – 10 indicate how you rated the session. (Circle the number that fits you)**

	Room for improvement									Excellent
1. The format was effective for me	1	2	3	4	5	6	7	8	9	10
2. The discussion was relevant to my needs	1	2	3	4	5	6	7	8	9	10
3. I can see how the interactive discussion was useful to me	1	2	3	4	5	6	7	8	9	10
4. Had the right amount of participation for me	1	2	3	4	5	6	7	8	9	10
5. I see how my role as a team member matters	1	2	3	4	5	6	7	8	9	10
6. I understand the role and responsibilities of my fellow staff members	1	2	3	4	5	6	7	8	9	10
7. I can see how the insights / ideas it gave me will make a difference in my work	1	2	3	4	5	6	7	8	9	10
8. I can see where/how I will take action immediately	1	2	3	4	5	6	7	8	9	10

2. **Some of the small steps I plan to take right away are:**

a.

b.

c.

3. **The facilitation of the meeting was helpful to me in the following two ways:**

a.

b.

4. **Suppose, the next committee/staff briefing discussion is even more effective, what one or two things might be different or enhance it?**

j) Some recipes for selling Solution Focus to a client or a team (author)

Finally, how do you sell Solution Focus?

Selling Solution Focus to a team isn't always easy, especially when working with a reluctant team. The counterintuitive aspect of asking, "What's working?" sometimes seems, at best, abstract.

People buy benefits first, features second. It's tempting to sell the features of solution focus because they are potentially so useful. Why not have them enjoy the benefits right away?

There are two parts to selling Solution Focus:

a. Selling the features.

b. Having the team sell it to themselves by experiencing the benefits of solution focus in the proposal process.

a) Selling the features.

Most teams' eyes glaze over when you go deep on the features, so less is more. However, some teams do need a lot of details.

Here's how to talk about Solution Focus in a way that works for the team:

When you (the team) are looking for change and/or are stuck, Solution Focus is a simple and efficient way to:

- arrange complex problems into manageable bits.

- develop your own insights and solutions.

- start or speed up change.

- free up resources that are being absorbed by the problem.

What makes it unique?

- you are the expert, so you build on your existing knowledge, skills, and resources.

- it changes your perspective from the present problem to a future desired solution.

The key elements are conversations to find out:

- what already works or worked in the past.

- what it will look like in the future when it is working well.

- what is the first small step forward you can take, building on what already works.

- what are the benefits.

- learning a new way of thinking that helps get what you want.

- speeds up the change process and change begins almost immediately.

- shifts time and resources to achieving your personal business goals.

- gets you out of the problem and on to implementing solutions with actions and accountabilities.

b) Having the team sell it to themselves by experiencing it in the proposal process

Most presentations and pitches are (unintentionally) one-way conversations. The presenter likely has limited knowledge of what the team is thinking. The team may also be uncertain about how much of the problem it is appropriate to share.

It is therefore essential to first open up communication by getting the team talking about their situation (well before the presenter makes his or her case). When telling their story, the team will reveal facts about themselves that the presenter can use to determine how best to be helpful.

Try to avoid presenting your ideas for as long as possible. Why? In order to get a clearer picture of what the team really needs. You may inadvertently present something they don't want by not first knowing their needs.

Once the team's perspective is clearer, it is important to downplay the presenter's expertise about the team's business: "We know just enough about your business to be able to apply our Solution Focus expertise and make a difference."

"Thinking of the problem you have outlined, what is working (in this area) that we don't have to change?" "What is it that the team is already good at?"

"Suppose we were helpful; what differences would you hope to see in your team after we had gone?"

"How would this outcome help you personally?"

"When you have worked with consultants / trainers / coaches before, what worked best?"

"Now that you have seen our thinking, could you tell me what sort of difference it might make (for you, for your team)?" (Probe for details.)

"How would this approach help you and your team move forward?" (Probe for details.)

"Given your thoughts on the concepts, can you tell me more about the situation you are facing?"
(Probe for details.)

"Now that we better understand your situation, how might we help you make a difference—right away?"

Contributors:

Andry Anastasiou, Team Training andry@teamtraining.org.uk

Helen Bailey: Pinna. Helen@pinna.co.uk

Michael Hjerth. michael@solutionwork.se

Kirsten Dierolf, SolutionsAcademy, Germany
kirsten@solutionsacademy.com

Carey Glass www.thehumancentre.co.uk

Paul Z Jackson, www.thesolutionsfocus.co.uk
paul@thesolutionsfocus.co.uk

Björn Johansson, www.clues.se

Jackie Keddy www.keddyconsultants.com

Shaun Lincoln: shaunlincoln@hotmail.com

Guenter Lueger www.solutionmanagement.at

Dr Mark McKergow PhD MBA, United Kingdom www.sfwork.com

Coert Visser: www.m-cc.nl

Janine Waldman: janine@thesolutionsfocus.co.uk

A thank you also goes to my partner Pauline Tice for her advice and
many affirmations about the quality of the ideas in this book.

Suggested resources:

ASFCT: www.asfct.org

SOLworld: www.solworld.ning.com

The Solutions Focus: www.thesolutionsfocus.com

Solutionsurfers: www.solutionsurfers.com

Coert Visser: www.m-cc.nl

Solutions Academy: www.solutionsacademy.com

For Insoo Kim Berg training downloads go to
www.sfbta.org (training/downloads)

About the author:

Alan Kay is a leader in solution focused application. He has helped many organizations focus on solutions by asking better questions so that they can re-frame problems into solutions. He notes that his clients, from banks to children's aid society, are the resource for change.

A former general manager in the marketing communications sector, his passion is to help clients focus on successful outcomes for their customers and stakeholders. He believes that organizational productivity increases can come from technology, but that people are the greatest source of opportunity, and that progress improvements and ROI will come from people who can collaborate cross-functionally on solutions for the customer.

Alan was first trained in Solution Focus in late 1990s at Brief Therapy Training Centres International (Hinks Dellcrest Centre) and has been applying it in areas of strategic planning, customer experience, stakeholder consultation, organizational development and many other areas.

Alan teaches at the Schulich School of Business, York University. He is a founding member of ASFCT, an association dedicated to quality development in Solution Focus and is a frequent contributor to conferences on Solution Focus in organizations.

He also quite likes monkeys.

Blog: www.sforganization.com

Website: www.glasgrp.com

13080466R00044

Made in the USA
Charleston, SC
15 June 2012